STRANGERS

PHOENIX POETS
A Series Edited by Robert von Hallberg

STRANGERS

A Book of Poems

David Ferry

THE UNIVERSITY OF CHICAGO PRESS
Chicago and London

DAVID FERRY is professor and chairman of the Department of English at Wellesley College. He is the author of *On the Way to the Island,* a collection of poems, and *The Limits of Mortality: An Essay on Wordsworth's Major Poems.*

The University of Chicago Press, Chicago 60637
The University of Chicago Press, Ltd., London

©1983 by The University of Chicago
All rights reserved. Published 1983
Printed in the United States of America

90 89 88 87 86 85 84 83   5 4 3 2 1

Library of Congress Cataloging in Publication Data

Ferry, David.
    Strangers: a book of poems.

    (Phoenix poets)
    I. Title.   II. Series.
PS3511.E74S8   1983   811′.54   83-1163
ISBN 0-226-24469-5
ISBN 0-226-24470-9 (pbk.)

For Elizabeth and Stephen Ferry

Think thou how that this is not our home in this world, in which we are strangers, one not knowing another's speech and language.

The Diary of Samuel Ward, entry for May 13, 1595

A number of the poems in this book have been published previously, in the following places:

The Blacksmith Anthology: "On Haystack Mountain," "A Walk in the Woods."
Boston University Graduate Journal: "The Waiting."
The New Republic: "A Tomb at Tarquinia," "To Sestius," "La Farandola dei Fanciulli," "Graveyard."
The Partisan Review: "Seen through a Window," "Several Voices."
Ploughshares: "At the Bus Stop; Eurydice," "Ellery Street," "My Mother's Dying," "On a Sunday Morning" (published also in *Poetry Amherst*), "After Spotsylvania Court House," "Evening News I," "Evening News II," "Sculptures by Dimitri Hadzi," "Rereading Old Writing."
Poetry: "Cythera," "A Night-Time River Road," "To Sally," "Photographs from a Book."
Poetry Miscellany: "Caprimulgidae."
Raritan: "Out at Lanesville," "In Balance."

Part Six was published in 1981 in a limited edition of 120 copies by the Sea Pen Press, Seattle, under the title *A Letter, And Some Photographs*.

Contents

ONE

A Tomb at Tarquinia

The two of us, on the livingroom couch,
An Etruscan couple,
Blindeyed to the new light let suddenly in;
Sitting among the things that belong to us,
The style of living familiar, and easy,
Nothing yet utterly lost.

Leapers and dolphins adorn the painted walls;
The sun is rising,
Or setting, over a blue Tyrrhenian Sea;
In the pictured cup the wine brims and glistens;
An unknown flower burns with odorless incense
The still air of the place.

At the Bus Stop; Eurydice

The old lady's face.
Who knows whose it was?
The bus slid by me.
Who in the world knows me?

She was amazed, amazed.
Can death really take me?
The bus went away.
It took the old lady away.

Ellery Street

How much too eloquent are the songs we sing:
nothing we tell will tell how beautiful is the body.

It does not belong
even to him or her who lives in it.

Beautiful the snail's body which it bears
laboriously in its way through the long garden.

The old lady who lives next door has terribly scarred legs.
She bears her body laboriously to the Laundromat.

There's a fat girl in the apartment across the street.
I can see her unhappiness in the flower she wears

in her hair; it blooms in her hair like a flower
in a garden, like a flower flowering in a dream

dreamed all night, a night–
blooming cereus. A boy passes by, his bare

chest flashing like a shield in the summer air;
all-conquering,

the king going to the drug store.
The snail crosses the garden in its dignified silence.

My Mother's Dying

I listen at the door.
Who's dying, then?
It's like bird-watching.

Who's going to die next?
Birds in the nest.
Who knows about all this?

Several Voices

the tall man
> Height scares me. I am always afraid of falling.
> The snaky sea lies coiled around my feet.
> When I fall down those snakes will ravin me.

the fat woman
> I billow on my bones. The axle of the world
> Bears seas about itself in its difficult turning.
> Where is this heavy world lumbering to?

the pretty girl
> The blossom on the stem, tossed on a sunny wind.
> The hummingbird and bee come to me for favor.
> Giving and taking, we're a whole act together.

the old sick man
> What scares me is the bright touch of a sharp point
> Of white light, piercing my dark.
> I prayed I'd go to sleep in that pitch dark.

A Night-Time River Road

We were driving down a road.
Where was it we were going?
Where were we going to?
Nobody knew.

Behind the blur of trees
Along the river road,
Somewhere behind the blur,
A dark river ran.

The car bore us along.
We didn't know who we were
Or where we were going to.
Somebody must know,

Somebody in the car
Must know where we were going,
Beside the dark river,
Where we were going to.

All silent in the car
We sat staring ahead.
Where were the lights of a bar,
A gas station, a house?

Out in the dark the river
Was telling itself a story.
There in the car nobody
Could tell where we were going.

TWO

On a Sunday Morning

It is a beauteous evening, calm and free

My child and I
Are walking around the block.
No sea heaves near. No anger
Blooms through the perfect sky.

The flashing of the wheels
Of a passing car is not
The flashing of that fate
I might have feared, not this Sunday.

A page from a newspaper
Drifts along the gutter.
It is a leaf
Fallen from a terrible tree,

The tree of anger,
Tears, fearfulness.
It is nothing to him,
And nothing to me, this Sunday.

Sculptures by Dimitri Hadzi

This metal blooms in the dark of Rome's
Day light. Of how many deaths
Is Rome the bright flowering?
See, the dead bloom in the dark
Of the Fosse Ardeatina. The black
Breath of the war has breathed on them;
Shields gleam, and helmets, in the memory.

Their flowering is their being true
To their own nature; not being
A glory, a victory; being a record,
The way things are in war.
In the nature of things the flowers grow
With the authority of telling the truth;
Their brightness is dark with it.

Evening News I

We have been there
          and seen nothing
Nothing has been there
          for us to see
In what a beautiful silence
          the death is inflicted
In a dazzling distance
          in the fresh dews
And morning lights
          how radiantly
In the glistening
          the village is wasted.
It is by such sights
          the eye is instructed

Evening News II

The face looking into the room;
Behind it light, shaking, like heat
Lightning; the face calm and knowing;
Seeing, but not seeing who I am;
The mouth may be telling something.

Something about our helplessness;
Something about the confusions of beasts;
The consequence of error; systems
Haywire, or working; the stars gone
All wrong in the body's courses.

Out on the plain of Mars, brilliantly
Played under the lights, searched out
Beyond any answer, the game went on
Far into the night; the bloodiest came
Home from the battle seeking the prize.

The women were disgraced; hair streaming,
Pleading into the staring; buy, buy—
Was it my daughter I was seeing?—
The humiliation was pleasing: tears,
Laughter, smiles, all mingled together.

The light swallowed itself, a balloon
Deflating; somewhere in the blackness
A murmuring let itself go.

THREE

Caprimulgidae

It makes its flight in the competence of its own
Way of behaving; hovering, or gliding,
Floating, oddly, just at the edges of bushes,
Just over the ground, or near the vagueness of trees,
At twilight, on the hunt for moths or other
Creatures out in the failing evening light.
It feeds while flying hugely, softly, smiling,
The gape open to far back under the ears;
In the dim air it looks like a giant moth,
Fluttering, the blurred disheveled feathers waving,
Signaling something that understands its meaning.

Its young are born unhelpless. Caprimulgus
Can totter or hop only a few steps,
Almost a cripple, its little legs so feeble;
Perhaps on the flat roof of some city building,
Or out on the bare ground, or on a tree-limb,
It lies all day, waking in its sleeping,
Capable, safe, concealed in its cryptic plumage,
Invisible to almost anything;
Its nightready eyes are closed, carefully
Keeping the brilliant secret of its flight;
Its hunting begins when the light begins to go.

A Charm

I have a twin who bears my name;
Bears it about with him in shame;

Who goes a way I would not go;
Has knowledge of things I would not know;

When I was brave, he was afraid;
He told the truth, I lied;

What's sweet to me tastes bitter to him;
My friends, my friends, he loves not them;

I walk the daylight in his dream;
He breathes the air of my nightmare.

On Haystack Mountain

I stand here, on the top of the mountain, here
In the dark, looking out over the night's darkness
As over a dark ocean. Even by day
The ocean's a kind of darkness, with all it conceals,
So the darkness, with all it conceals, is a kind of ocean.

I look up at the night sky, picked out with all
Its stars. How clear, how clear, in a cold how clear
Society of love. Peacefulness, quietness,
The dark spaces between the bright stars . . .

In my unquestioning heart is some restful grief
Or pleasure, here in the dark, on the mountain,
Under the famous stars, here in my sole self,
For once not anxious or sorry, contending for now
Not at all with anger, ambition, pity . . .

The Waiting

Someone hammering something somewhere outside;
The sound of the plumbing faithfully dying away
Somewhere in the building; the ocean noises of cars
From blocks beyond, like the quiet breathing of waves;
The mad young woman waits for her faithful lover;
Her innocent curtains tell her the secrets of summer air.

She stands at her window and waits; somewhere outside
Someone is hammering something; the ocean is breathing;
The mailman has come and gone, he spoke her name;
The curtains whisper a little against the sill;
How often he comes to her door, the imposter, her lover;
He speaks in a secret tongue understood by no other.

Table Talk

How can he stand it,
Being talked about that way?
His every madness the subject
Of every dinner table
Talk that's unworthy of him?

I saw his wife on the street,
Her mouth showing the pain
Of the self-discipline
His trouble imposes on her.
What is it for, all the talk?

I saw his daughter, too,
Small, ordinary, charming.
What will it be for her?
Madness cries out too loudly.
The pain is too much to bear.

God bless unthinking living.
God bless this house and all
Those who live within it.

Cythera

There they go, down to the fatal ship.
They know how beautiful they are.
The ship will sail very soon. The sea
Will cover them over very soon unknowingly.

Wave goodbye from the shore, children.
I can see how your faces change in the sight
Of their going away. Wave to them.

Their sails are of silk, they're very pretty.
The sunset is all smiles, radiance,
The hues of a first or last innocence.
You look hungry, children, tired, angry.

Very beautiful is the manner of their going.
Music is playing about the mast; their lovely faces
Look lovelier still compared to the angry children.

In Eden

You lie in our bed as if an orchard were over us.
You are what's fallen from those fatal boughs.
Where will we go when they send us away from here?

A Walk in the Woods

Sweet bird, whose song, like all natural things,
Is but the saying aloud of what is withheld from me,
The knowledge of what it means,

I have known times when one who is dear to me
Spoke to say something as lovely as what the sweet bird sings,
Alone, in a green thicket.

Seen through a Window

A man and a woman are sitting at a table.
It is supper time. The air is green. The walls
Are white in the green air, as rocks under water
Retain their own true color, though washed in green.
I do not know either the man or the woman,
Nor do I know whatever they know of each other.
Though washed in my eye they keep their own true color.

The man is all his own hunched strength, the body's
Self and strength, that bears, like weariness,
Itself upon itself, as a stone's weight
Bears heavily on itself to be itself.
Heavy the strength that bears the body down.
And the way he feeds is like a dreamless sleep;
The dreaming of a stone is how he feeds.

The woman's arms are plump, mottled a little
The flesh, like standing milk, and on one arm
A blue bruise, got in some household labor or other,
Flowering in the white. Her staring eye,
Like some bird's cry called from some deepest wood,
Says nothing of what it is but what it is.
Such silence is the bird's cry of a stone.

Out at Lanesville

In memoriam Mary Ann, 1932–1980

The five or six of them, sitting on the rocks
Out at Lanesville, near Gloucester; it is like
Listening to music. Several of them are teachers,
One is a psychologist, one is reading a book,
The page glares white in the summer sunlight;
Others are just sunning themselves, or just
Sitting there looking out over the water;
A couple of them seem to be talking together;
From this far off you can't hear what they are saying.

The day is hot, the absolute middle of summer.
Someone has written an obscenity
In huge letters on the rocks above and behind
This group of people, and someone else, one of them,
Maybe, or maybe a neighbor, the owner of one
Of the cottages up behind and back in the woods,
Has tried to erase it and only partly done so,
So that for years it will say hoarsely FUCK
To the random winds and to the senseless waves.

One of them is sitting with her back turned
To me and to the others on the rocks. The purple
Loosestrife and the tigerlilies are like the flags
Of some celebration; they bloom along the edge
Of a small stream that makes its way unseen
Down to the rocks and sand. Her shoulders are round,
And rather luxuriously heavy, and the whole figure
Has a youthful and graceful amplitude of being
Whose beauty will last her her whole life long.

The voices of some people out in a boat somewhere
Are carried in over the water with surprising
Force and clarity, though saying I don't know what:
Happiness. Unhappiness. Something about the conditions
Of all such things. Work done, not done. The saving
Of the self in the intense work of its singleness,
Learning to live with it. Their lives have separate ends.
Suddenly she turns her head and seems to look
Towards me and towards the others on the rocks,

So that her body, turned away, is more expressive
Than her blank face, like a pure reflector of light.

FOUR

To Sestius

Horace *Odes* 1.4

Now the hard winter is breaking up with the welcome coming
   Of spring and the spring winds; some fishermen,
Under a sky that looks changed, are hauling their caulked boats
   Down to the water; in the winter stables the cattle
Are restless; so is the farmer sitting in front of his fire;
   They want to be out of doors in field or pasture;
The frost is gone from the meadowgrass in the early mornings.
   Maybe, somewhere, the nymphs and graces are dancing,
Under the moon the goddess Venus and her dancers;
   Somewhere far in the depth of a cloudless sky
Vulcan is getting ready the storms of the coming summer.
   Now is the time to garland your shining hair
With myrtle and with the flowers the free-giving earth has given:
   Now is the right time to offer the kid or lamb
In sacrifice to Faunus in the firelit shadowy grove.

Revenant whitefaced death is walking not knowing whether
   He's going to knock at a rich man's door or a poor man's.
Oh goodlooking fortunate Sestius, don't put your hope in the future;
   The night is falling; the shades are gathering around;
The walls of Pluto's shadowy house are closing you in;
   There who will be lord of the feast? What will it matter,
What will it matter, there, whether you fell in love
   With Lycidas, this or that girl with him, or he with her?

La Farandola dei Fanciulli

after Eugenio Montale

How far back the ancient past seems now.
Those kids dancing around and playing,
By the railroad track, up back of the beach,
On the gravel and cinders of the railbed,

Weeds suddenly breaking into blossom
In the heat of the day, a flowering of thirst.
It's as if being naked and nameless
Was being sunlight, flower, heat-shimmer.

In Balance

after Jorge Guillen

I am so happy. It is wonderful
To breathe the air and be in the morning light.
On a day like this, if the soul weighs anything
It is like the weight of a flower bending itself
Down to the earth in the weightless light and air.

Everything calmly gives itself up
To happiness on a day like this. The whiteness
Of a wall gives whiteness to the eye that looks at it.
The grass in the vacant lot across the street
Yields to the morning breeze that flows across it,

Till the breeze dies down like the end of a sentence spoken.

FIVE

A Telephone Call

A strong smell of dog, of my dog's death;
My old dog is lying there, giving me lessons in dying;
I talked to my father, my father called me tonight:
The sour breath of the telephone telling the truth.

At the Hospital

How beautiful she'd become:
Strange fish,
In that aquarium;
Rare find,
She swam in that element,
In the body's knowledge.

To Sally

Now we've been sitting up all night,
Waiting to find out
What the story is.

I watch your beautiful patient face:
It's as if you didn't know
All that you know.

Your mother in mortal danger, you speak
Of something funny that happened.
What will have happened,

Maybe, before your story's finished?
Good people are punished
Like all the rest.

At the Hospital

She was the sentence the cancer spoke at last,
Its blurred grammar finally clarified.

SIX

After Spotsylvania Court House

I read the brown sentences of my great-grandfather,
As if—not even as if, but actually—
Looking into a brown photograph as old
As his writing is. In his sentences
Two innocent naked young men, Methodists,
Bathe in the morning in the Rapahannock River,
At Fredericksburg, Virginia, eighteen sixty-four.
Brother Pierson and I went out and bathed in the Rapahannock.
Returned to take our breakfast on coffee and bread.
I can see the young men bathing in those sentences,
And taking their breakfast, in the letter home.
We sat down on the clean grass, in the Garden;
Around us strawberries, cherries, gooseberries, currants
Were ripening, though not yet ready for use . . .

An unluxurious incense, intense, dry, pure,
Rises from this letter and from his life.
The morning air seemed to take up the song of our praise.
It is a wonderful honor to be here and to do good.
The river is flowing past the hospital,
Nearly as wide as the Delaware at Trenton,
And like it shallow. I can see the young men walking
Through the early streets, on the way to the hospital,
With paper and jellies and clothing, all laden down.
The morning vapor is rising from the river.
There were about 200, some of them so young.
We wrote letters for them, bound up wounds, prepared
Delicacies. We prayed, and sang "A Charge to Keep."
The incense has the odor of old paper.

Photographs from a Book: Six Poems

I

A poem again, of several parts, each having to do
With a photograph. The first, by Eakins, is of his student,
Samuel C. Murray, about twenty-five years old,
Naked, a life study, in the cold light and hungry
Shadow of Eakins's studio in Philadelphia.
The picture was taken in eighteen ninety-two.
The young man's face is unsmiling, shy, or appears to be so
Because of the shadow. One knows from other
Images in the book that Murray's unshadowed gaze
Can look out clear, untroubled, without mystery or guile.
His body is easy in its selfhood, in its self and strength;
The virtue of its perfection is only of its moment
In the light and shadow. In the stillness of the photograph
I cannot see the light and shadow moving
As light and shadow move in the moving of a river.

II

He stands against what looks like the other side
Of a free-standing bookcase, with a black cloth
Draped over it, and a shelf as the top of it,
And on the shelf, sad, some bits and pieces
Of old 'fine' culture and bric-a-brac:
An urn; a child's head; a carved animal
Of some sort, a dog or a wolf, it's hard to tell;
A bust of a goddess staring out at nothing;
Something floral in wood or plaster. "The Arcadians
Are said to have inhabited the earth
Before the birth of Jupiter; their tribe
Was older than the moon. Not as yet enhanced
By discipline or manners, their life
Resembled that of beasts; they were an uncouth
People, who were still ignorant of art."

III

There is a strange, solemn, silent, graceless
Gayety in their dancing, the dancing of the young
Ladies of Philadelphia in the anxious
Saffron light of Eakins's photograph;
There in the nineteenth century, dressed in their 'Grecian'
Long white dresses, so many years ago,
They are dancing or standing still before the camera,
Selfhood altered to an alien poetry,
The flowers in their hair already fading;
Persephone, Dryope, Lotis, or maybe only
Some general Philadelphia notion of Grecian
Nymph or maiden, posing, there by the river.
"If those who suffer are to be believed,
I swear by the gods my fate is undeserved."
The light in Eakins's photograph is ancient.

IV

Plate 134. By Eakins. "A cowboy in the West.
An unidentified man at the Badger Company Ranch."
His hat, his gun, his gloves, his chair, his place
In the sun. He sits with his feet in a dried-up pool
Of sunlight. His face is the face of a hero
Who has read nothing at all about heroes.
He is without splendor, utterly without
The amazement of self that glorifies Achilles
The sunlike, the killer. He is without mercy
As he is without the imagination that he is
Without mercy. There is nothing to the East of him
Except the camera, which is almost entirely without
Understanding of what it sees in him,
His hat, his gun, his gloves, his homely and
Heartbreaking canteen, empty on the ground.

V

The Anasazi drink from underground rivers.
The petroglyph cries out in the silence of the rock
The tourist looks at. The past is beautiful.
How few the implements and how carefully made
The dwelling place, against the wind and heat.
Looking at a photograph, as at a petroglyph,
How little there is to go on. "The darkest objects
Reflect almost no light, or none at all,
Causing no changes in the salts in the emulsion."
In the brilliant light and heart-stifling heat,
The scratchings on the surface of the rock,
Utterings, scriptions, bafflings of the spirit,
The bewildered eye reads nonsense in the dazzle;
In the black depth of the rock the river says nothing,
Reflectionless, swift, intent, purposeless, flowing.

VI

A picture of Eakins and a couple of other people,
One of them Murray, bathing in a river,
The Cohansey, near Fairton, New Jersey; Eakins
An old man, Murray no longer young; the other man,
Elderly, smiling, "probably Charlie Boyers."
They are patiently waiting for the picture to be taken.
It is a summer evening. The photograph
Is overexposed, so the light and the water are almost
Impossible to distinguish one from the other,
In their mutual weakness; an oarless rowboat waits
In the water, just clear of the rivergrass and weeds;
The opposite bank of the river is hard to see
In the washy blankness of the light; the sallow
Flat South Jersey landscape, treeless almost,
Almost featureless, stretches vaguely beyond.

Graveyard

A writing I can't read myself: the picture
Of my father, taken a couple of years
Before he died; he is sitting alone some place
I don't know; maybe one of the meetings
He took to going to, trying to keep
His place in the world; he is smiling a little,
Cigarette smoke drifting away; he looks
Courteous, as always, not easy to know.

The side of a hill, nothing but a place;
Grass, dirt, a few scattered sticks, some stones,
The shadow of a tree; *Eurydice,*
My father; speaking the words as they are spoken
The meaning closes itself up; a manuscript
Written in a language only the dead speak.

Counterpart

The last poem in this section of the book,
A counterpart to the one my great-grandfather
Wrote lines of, in his letter home: the ripening
Fruit, the purity of intention and deed
In the context of blood and error, the river
That has flowed in every man's ear from generation
To generation. When my great-grandfather preached,
One day, "a wonderful visitation of the Holy Spirit
Came down upon the church. It seemed to fall
On men and women in different parts of the congregation
Until upon all there was one baptism
Of the Holy Fire, and he was thus in his little church
Consecrated to God in the work of preaching."
I found the letter in a metal box in my dead father's

Apartment; the place was shadowy even in the daytime;
Mild, early in September; quiet outside
On the street, and in the apartment; the television
Going, the sound turned off, images flickering
And fluttering inside the lighted screen,
Shaking and gesturing, beseeching the attention.
The ink of the faded ancient writing
Flowed across the page, flowed and lapsed, lapsed
Into forgetfulness: the morning air, the blankness
Of the light, a vapor, a shadow moving,
An unidentified man, selfhood altered.
"I am a child of the earth and of the sky.
But give me quickly the cold water to drink
That flows from Memory's source, from Lebadeia."

SEVEN

Rereading Old Writing

Looking back, the language scribbles.
What's hidden, having been said?
Almost everything? Thrilling to think
There was a secret there somewhere,
A bird singing in the heart's forest.

Two people sitting by a river;
Sunlight, shadow, some pretty trees;
Death dappling in the flowing water;
Beautiful to think about,
Romance inscrutable as music.

Out of the ground, in New Jersey, my mother's
Voice, toneless, wailing—beseeching?
Crying out nothing? A winter vapor,
Out of the urn, rising in the yellow
Air, an ashy smear on the page.

The quiet room floats on the waters,
Buoyed up gently on the daylight;
The branch I can see stirs a little;
Nothing to think about; writing
Is a way of being happy.

What's going to be in this place?
A person entering a room?
Saying something? Signaling?
Writing a formula on a blackboard.
Something not to be understood.

Notes

"Epigraph"
   The epigraph is quoted from *Two Elizabethan Puritan Diaries,* ed. Marshall M. Knappen (Chicago: American Society of Church History, 1933), p. 103.

"Sculptures by Dimitri Hadzi"
   In reprisal for the killing of 32 German soldiers by the *Resistenza* in Rome, the Germans gathered together 335 Romans, representing all classes, ages, and occupations, and slaughtered them in the Ardeatine Caves on March 24, 1944.

"Caprimulgidae"
   Information and some phraseology are taken from several ornithological books, most particularly from John Gooders, *The Great Book of Birds* (New York: Dial, 1975).

"Out at Lanesville"
   "Their lives have separate ends" is a quotation from Longfellow's great poem "The Fire of Drift-wood."

"After Spotsylvania Court House"
   The battle took place May 8–11, 1864.
   "A Charge to Keep" is no. 388 in *The Methodist Hymnal.*
   The quotations in this poem are from a letter of Joseph H. Knowles to his wife, Ellin J. Knowles, May 23, 1864.

"Photographs from a Book: Six Poems"
   Several of the photographs evoked in the poems are related to photographs reproduced in *The Photographs of Thomas Eakins,* ed. Gordon Hendricks (New York: Grossman, 1972). The quotations in poems IV and VI are from notes to photographs in this book.
   The quotation in poem II, lines 9–15, is from Ovid *Fasti,* 2.289ff., as translated in Erwin Panofsky, *Meaning in the Visual Arts* (New York: Doubleday, 1955), p. 299.

The quotation in poem III, lines 13–14, is from Ovid *Metamorphoses* 9.371–73.

The Anasazi, referred to in poem V, line 1, are the "Old People," prehistoric Indians of the Southwest. The quotation in poem V, lines 7–9, is paraphrased from the article "Photography" in *The World Book Encyclopedia* (1966 edition), 15:380.

"Counterpart"

The quotation in lines 8–13 is from an obituary article on Joseph H. Knowles in a Methodist journal from 1898.

Lines 26–28—these and similar verses are found on the so-called Orphic Gold Leaf fragments. See Gunther Zuntz, *Persephone* (New York: Oxford University Press, 1971), pp. 277–93, and Emily Vermeule, *Aspects of Death in Early Greek Art and Poetry* (Berkeley: University of California Press, 1979), p. 58.

Lebadeia is the place of an oracle, near the sources of Lethe and Mnemosyne.